YORKSHIRE VILLAGES

YORKSHIRE VILLAGES

TRAVELS THROUGH DALES AND MOORS · PAUL BARKER

—— FOREWORD BY ——
MICHAEL PARKINSON

—— COMMENTARY BY ——
JAMES BIRDSALL

PARKGATE
BOOKS

First published by Pavilion Books Limited, 1992
This edition published in 1998 by

Parkgate Books Ltd
Kiln House
210 New King's Road
London SW6 4NZ
Great Britain

1 3 5 7 9 8 6 4 2

British Library Cataloguing in Publication Data:
A catalogue record for this book is available from the British Library.

ISBN 1 85585 542 9

Designed by Andrew Barrow & Collis Clements Associates

Printed and bound in China
by Sun Fung Offset Binding Company Limited.
Produced in association with the Hanway Press, London.

Page 1: Hinchcliffe Mill
Page 3: Kettlewell

HONLEY

CONTENTS

As a child I looked out across fields of corn and meadow to the pit. There was the long slag heap, the pit head gear against the sky and the red brick houses poking out from the pit top. Down the road made from coal dust where we walked to the pit there were hawthorn hedgerows full of nesting birds. There were rabbits and pheasants near the spot where they dumped the waste to make another mountain of muck. It was a strange juxtaposition of countryside and industry. You won't find many pictures of the village where I lived in this book, but the fact is that wherever you are in Yorkshire the beguiling charms of its landscape are never far away.

Some of the villages in the book we used to visit on our bikes when we were kids. They were where the posh people lived, people who owned the mines but didn't work in them. Later on these were the villages with the timbered pubs where we took our lady friends and ordered cocktails, the names of which we heard on American movies. I once ordered a 'Highball' in a village pub near Barnsley and spent three days on my back recovering from alcohol poisoning. I wasn't served a Highball, but the barman's revenge for being uppity.

Since I moved away from Barnsley I have discovered the other parts of Yorkshire you see on the television, in the tourist guides and in this book. It is breathtakingly beautiful, mysterious and beguiling. Paul Barker has brought a skilled and sympathetic eye to his task and James Birdsall's commentary gives a flavour of the people who live in Yorkshire.

It is a common misconception – but not one that Mr Birdsall falls for – that all Yorkshiremen are alike. It is true they have several common characteristics like their love of good ale, cricket and the road leading out of Lancashire. But there are differences of dialect and attitudes within the county. People who live in Harrogate have little in common with folk who live in Barnsley, who can't understand what they say in Sheffield, who think that people in Scarborough talk funny, who think that folk who live on top of the moors where the trees are bent like old men and the wind is enough to cut you in two, must be crackers.

The charm of Yorkshire is that within its boundaries there are many tribes. There are also many landscapes and all of them are wonderfully captured in this book. If you visit Yorkshire you will soon become aware of the pride that people have in their county. This book demonstrates why. The traveller will also not have been long in the county before

HAWES

someone tells him that Yorkshire is England's biggest county and that there are more acres in Yorkshire than words in the Bible. Don't argue because it was certain to be a Yorkshireman who did the counting. What you will soon realise is that you don't measure Yorkshire, you experience it. What follows will show you what I mean.

Michael Parkinson

MIDDLESMOOR

ACKNOWLEDGEMENTS

Among many old friends and new acquaintances I would like to thank especially
my wife, Wendy, a Yorkshire villager, and Dave the Fireman,
who between them ferried me over eleven hundred miles
in the course of writing this book, and Joe Smith, Dalesman,
who from the depths of his extensive knowledge of
Yorkshire lore and folk-history lent me a hand (he has only the one).

Jas Birdsall

> . . . As one who long in populous city pent
> Where houses thick and sewers annoy the air
> Forth issuing on a summer's morn to breathe
> Amongst the pleasant villages and farms
> Adjoin'd, from each thing met conceives delight.

Milton, *Paradise Lost*

THE VERY AIR is sniffed proprietorially in the Yorkshire countryside, a source of pride along with Yorkshire pudding, mint pasty and pork pies with mushy peas. Often my brothers and I used to stay with my grandparents in their little Wharfedale village, roam unrestricted and eat ravenously. 'It's the Yorkshire air,' my grandmother would say complacently. 'It gives everyone an appetite.' That it owed much also to her scrumptious Yorkshire cooking never seemed to occur to her.

Villages are man-made, however much, as in Yorkshire notably, they seem to spring from the landscape. Until the advent of the railways, building materials in the north were for generations hewn from the close hillside and cut from the local woodland, as near to the site as possible. The ensuing barns, farms and houses, unregulated and random, huddling together for comfort, have been toughened and annealed like their occupants by centuries of stern weather. Lichens and algae have long ago reclaimed the bright surfaces of raped stone, and the buildings melt into the scree and fell whence they were conceived. Cities, towns and ancient abbeys boast their varied beauties of architecture, but the charm of the Yorkshire villages lies in this disposition to blend into the prospect.

The prospects are handsome, varying quickly as you travel, from dale to dale, from pale limestone through ochreous sandstone to dark millstone grit, their grace treasured, albeit inarticulately, by the residents. I was painting years ago the sweeping panorama from a cluster of farm buildings on the Howgill Fells and the shepherd eyed my work over my shoulder in passing.

'Tha's making a real job of that!'

'What a beautiful view you have here,' I replied.

'Nay, lad,' he said tersely, 'I know nowt about beauty.'

Then he added, brightening, 'But I'm a bugger for scenery!' The word is an inoffensive one in Yorkshire, and I know just what he meant. I feel exactly the same.

Villages are constantly evolving, along with their way of life. In the latter half of our century, increased mechanization and efficient transport have revolutionized agricultural methods and drastically reduced the workforce. Arrogantly lush rye grass, uniformly viridian and chemically fertilized, is now cut early for silage. The old hay meadows are rare and the battalions of haymakers extinct. In consequence the meadow flowers are disappearing and the ground nesting birds, partridge, curlew, lapwing, skylark, who could once calculate on raising their broods before the hay was cut, have largely left the pastures as the descendants of the farming families have left the villages.

Nature abhors a vacuum. Folk from the industrial towns and cities flock nose-to-tail in their cars to the countryside for weekends and bank holidays. Most recently the hysterical boom in the property market, the north lagging behind the south, has encouraged the mushroom growth of holiday homes, barn conversions and picturesque retreats for the retired, many of the 'offcomed 'uns' having migrated northwards. We have not had a true Yorkshire winter for a decade, and I suspect there are surprises in store for some. The effect on village life has been cataclysmic. Young members of families whose village roots go back for centuries cannot afford to set up house where their ancestors lived. Other villagers, lured by the inflated prices of their homes, have sold up and gone. On the credit side, the shabbiness of villages whose livelihood had been eroded has given place to renewed pride in appearance as the B&B signs multiply and a more leisured community replaces the old.

Such upheavals have happened throughout the past, often far more violently. Records of changing populations remain in the names of the villages, mostly in the tail end. Marauding Vikings in the ninth and tenth centuries settled all over Yorkshire. The suffix -thwaite (as in Slaithwaite, Langthwaite, Yockenthwaite) derives from a Norse word meaning a clearing or paddock. Similarly -by (Bellerby, Flasby, Hawnby) denotes a farm or a village, whereas -thorpe (Grewelthorpe, Tibthorpe, Agglethorpe) was a hamlet or minor settlement. Earlier the Anglo-Saxons invaded from Europe from the fifth to the seventh centuries and bequeathed us -ton (Skipton, Grassington, Linton), a village or farmstead – not a town, surprisingly; -den (Buckden, Hebden, Luddenden), small valley; and -ham (Clapham, Meltham, Malham), dry ground rising from a marsh or river bend. Even earlier, before the Romans came, the Celts left us Old English clues such as -ley (Bradley, Honley, Ilkley), a wood; -wick (Austwick, Giggleswick, Hawkswick), a dairy farm; and -worth (Haworth, Oakworth, Hawksworth), an enclosure.

Above all, villages are people. Go to the church for the history then go to the pub for the myths (as a writer I feel that accuracy should never be allowed to spoil a good story). Here you will find the old-timers who remember the old ways and days, when cattle were brown and short horned, not black and white and bald, and were iron shod for the long walk to market. I still have a pair of cowshoes above my front door, handed down through three generations, artefacts which puzzle most of my visitors. You will hear how the grass was mown by horse and men, and the hay brought down by horse and sled; how sheep and shepherd would often perish in the struggle against the winter snows. But ever and again the subject will revert to people, the past characters, the time-honoured eccentrics, the stuff of legend and village lore, so often, so inaccurately, so inadequately termed 'ordinary people'.

Of course there is a host of famous people whose birthplaces lie in the Broad Acres. One thinks of artists in their craft such as Thomas Chippendale, the Brontës and Delius, and of villains such as Guy Fawkes who tried to blow up Parliament and Sir Philip Snowden who disgraced it by being the first Chancellor to put up the price of beer. A party of American tourists once quizzed the sexton, quietly working among the ancient tombstones of Bolton Priory.

'Do you meet any ghosts in pursuit of your occupation?' After his gaze had taken in the graves, the ruins, the woods and the moor and settled on his earnest inquisitor, his eventual reply left a world of speculation.

'Nobbut odd 'un!'

Jas Birdsall
Grassington, July 1991

HOOTON PAGNELL

Just off the A1 motorway near
Doncaster, set in unexpected
fields and woodland above the
coalmines, old cottages at ancient
Hooton Pagnell appear to grow
out of the rock to which the
village clings. A steep flight of
steps climbs to the church,
perched well above the road.
Much of the building is Norman,
possibly even the historic door,
still on its original hinges.

STAINBOROUGH

One of Yorkshire's many surprises, Stainborough lies quietly in a green, fertile oasis below Wentworth Castle in the dour coal mining district surrounding Barnsley. To Horace Walpole, the eighteenth-century castle, with its lake and temple, was 'one of the noblest houses in England'. Its park also contains a mock castle, one of the follies so fashionable in its day. Nearby are the remains of Rockley Abbey, its tower now incorporated into a farm. Into a Stainborough farming family in the mid-eighteenth century, one of five brothers, Joseph Bramah the inventor was born, destined to give the world the hydraulic press.

JACKSON BRIDGE

Jackson Bridge is a precipitous little village. The stone houses sit squarely on each other's shoulders. The pub at the bottom stubbornly prevents them all tumbling like dominoes into the stream below. Though some miles from Holmfirth (the magic of the television camera brings it almost next-door to Norah Batty's) the White Horse Inn will be instantly recognizable to devotees of *The Last of the Summer Wine*. Here I met Mr Edward Beever, whose family history contains a sad event.

Nearby Hepworth was the furthermost point reached by the Great Plague, blamed on a tea-chest of clothes dispatched from London to the Beevers. The story is probable, as the disease is flea-carried and 'visitors' may well have travelled in the clothes. The entire village was wiped out. In Jackson Bridge is a stone triangle, one of several marking the communal graves.

CAWTHORNE

The lungs of the collieries lie in little pockets of unravaged countryside. Among such is Cawthorne, four miles from Barnsley. Cannon Hall stands in almost 200 acres of fine parkland and it is now a Country House Museum. Here is the famous longbow traditionally ascribed to Little John. A more modest museum is in the village, created from two small cottages, timbered inside, on a ledge above the road. This contains village relics of the distant and not-too-distant past, from coal fossils to one of Hitler's bombs. Near the church is an intriguing stone drinking fountain, closely entwined with squirming dragons. Many of the old cottages have carved stones in their walls, and the churchyard wall incorporates interesting old coffin lids.

WOLFSTONES

This high, untamed moorland, well over a thousand feet above the valley of the young River Don, was described in 1379 as an area tenanted by 'wolves, deer and other wild animals'. The hamlet of Wolfstones is one claimant to being the site where the last wolf in England was killed. Just north of Kinder Scout and the High Peak District of Derbyshire, the view here looks towards Black Hill, the radio masts of Holme Moss and the Snake Pass, always in the news as the first Pennine road to be blocked when the snows come.

HINCHCLIFFE MILL

Not every village conforms to an idyllic picture of Dingley Dell and pastoral bliss. Villages grew in the main for utilitarian reasons and their charm is accidental. Hinchcliffe Mill evolved with the weaving industry and it has an undeniable charm of its own. The factory clock seems to have stopped. Most of the old terraced houses are four storeys high, their windows severely symmetrical, their shapes rectangular, purposeful. And yet there is a rightness; an echo of clogs and a glimpse of aprons and shawls. Seen from a distance, against the trees and the undulating moorland, the severity makes the picture become logical, its composition in unerring accord.

HOLME

Holme is a straggling, charming little village of neat gritstone houses. The Graveship of Holme, by ancient charter, grants free peat to its residents. Some still burn it, an aromatic bonus to the impressive panorama of fell and wooded moorland, hill farms, ghylls and wild pasture in which the village is snugly set. There is a sturdy herd of Highland cattle, their russet weatherproof shagginess contrasting markedly with the svelte black-and-white of the large, ubiquitous Friesians who have virtually eclipsed all other dairy breeds ('Nowt but gurt wattercans,' commented a disillusioned farmer who remembers the shorthorn herds) A datestone above the door of the Sunday School was carved in 1694. Compare this with Underhill House. Mr Arthur Quarmby, architect, built his modern home at Holme underground, the innocent looking turf above concealing even a swimming bath. The day of the Hobbit may yet arrive.

HINCHCLIFFE MILL

MELTHAM MILLS

Meltham Mills has an ancient heritage, farming and weaving, set doggedly in windswept moorland. The church dates from the middle of the seventeenth century, but Iron Age settlements predate it by a thousand years. The picture illustrates our more recent Scrap-Iron Age.

HOLME

HONLEY

Amid staggering countryside, Honley, renowned for its male-voice choir, was the site of a furious battle during the Civil War. Eerily the acrid smell of ball and powder seems to linger in steep, narrow cobbled streets and worn flagged pavements. One-storeyed shops, stone roofs sagging at the ridges like old horses, survive under austere Victorian buildings, built from the prosperous textile trade. Tony Heap told me that eleven Heap families were crofters in 1800 at Honley and neighbouring Oldfield. Windows surrounding the top storey of New Hagg (Norse for hilltop) Farm lit the family hand looms. Before the mills instituted collective labour, small crofters worked from sheep's back to woven cloth. Commercial acids were not then available for de-greasing the wool. A capacious barrel stood outside the entrance, into which the chamber-pots were emptied. As a gesture of courtesy, visiting gentlemen were expected to top it up on arrival. In this economical astringent the fleeces were scoured.

FARNLEY TYAS

Farnley Tyas is in 'Summer Wine' country, just south of Huddersfield. The 'clearing among the ferns', it roosts high above the woollen district amid spectacular rolling countryside, of woods, pastures and arable land. Prominent in the landscape is the eyecatching folly on Castle Hill seen distantly from Honley in the photograph on page 28. Here the view is even more stunning. From the top of the castle or, for the less adventurous, from the windows of the inn below it, the countryside is spread to view like a map, a patchwork of textile mills and moors, coal-mines and farmland, knitted into one homogeneous quilt.

MARSDEN

Though undeniably industrial,
Marsden, deep in a valley, is
surrounded by superb moorland
scenery. The approach over
Standedge reaches 1,300 feet but
the 'navigators' of the last century
tunnelled through for three miles
to bring canal and railway, deep
under heather and bracken, farms
and glens, and a mesolithic
settlement. Below an old mill by
the church, a packhorse bridge
recalls the days of a far earlier
means of goods transport. One
mill-owner was murdered by the
Luddites for his use of new-
fangled machine technology.
James Wolfe, who captured
Quebec, was born here at the
vicarage. The 'Railway' is a pub
full of nostalgic memorabilia to
excite the steam enthusiast. One
peremptory plaque on a necessary
door has its origins with the
Jubilee Candle and Tallow Co. It
dictates: 'No more than 3 persons
at a time are allowed in this privy.
By Order.'

SLAITHWAITE

With ingrained Yorkshire
economy, Slaithwaite is
pronounced 'Slowitt' by all but the
incurably posh. Textile mills
flourished here, and pioneering
industry built first the canal and
then the railway side by side with
the River Colne and threw two
imposing viaducts over the deep
valley. Wildness is never far away,
and by contrast, the broad sweep
of Slaithwaite Moor, home to few
save sheep, gives little indication
of the bustle of life below. Modern
technology, outsoaring the mill
chimneys, has seen the erection of
the sky-scraping broadcasting
masts of Moorside Edge. The
Britannia Mills were once the
paternalistic manorial mill of the
Kaye family, of the type
immortalized by Thomas
Armstrong and satirized by *Brass*,
when the rumour of 'trouble at
t'Mill' used to cause anxious
concern. The mill still preserves
much interesting old machinery
from those days.

LUDDENDEN

Luddenden is difficult to find, but the search is rewarding. Set in a steep hill, guarded by hills even steeper, it is a little labyrinth of sharp corners and narrow streets, cobbles cascading like waterfalls. In the centre of the maze stands the church by the beck, its tower tucked well below the highest old stone houses. An underground passage from the graveyard, now timorously bricked up, led to the cellar of the inn, the 'White Swan' until Trafalgar; since the victory it has been the 'Lord Nelson'. Its library was used by Branwell Brontë, who worked here. A barmaid was abducted by cavaliers during the frequent skirmishes here between Parliament and the Royalists. It still rankles. The pub has the annual duty of electing, on 12 June, the Lord Mayor of Luddenden, a signal honour involving the purchase of many pints for his charges. Beware of opening a little old oak chest!

HEPTONSTALL

In a region of wild moors, menaced by crags and deep ravines, Heptonstall perches on a high ridge above the valley of the River Calder. Once an important centre of the handloom weaving trade, its steep, narrow streets, cobbled to give firm footing to the laden packhorses, zigzag between dark stone houses in a compelling atmosphere of Old Yorkshire. Weavers' Square overlooks the churchyard of two churches, one thirteenth-century, ruined but warmly romantic, the other upright and sternly Victorian. The Tudor Grammar School now houses a museum in Churchyard Bottom and beneath the old Co-op are much older dungeons. Heptonstall also boasts the oldest Methodist church still in use; a curiously octagonal chapel, its foundation stone was laid by John Wesley 1764. Centuries before that, Paulinus climbed up here to preach in the course of his mission to convert King Edwin to Christianity.

BOOTH

Scarcely a village, but a twin row of old terraced weavers' cottages, Booth clings on to the flank of a ravine in the hills above the Calder valley. The picture looks down on the old Jowler Mill, 'bosom'd high in tufted trees', which once spun cotton and silk. It is perhaps surprising, within walking distance of the industrial warrens of Sowerby Bridge and Halifax, to find such tracts of unspoilt countryside where hard-driven toilers in the Victorian textile mills could escape momentarily from the smoke and breathe a cleaner air.

HAWORTH

Haworth is a place of pilgrimage rather than beauty, of laboriously steep cobbled streets, of the ghosts of felled mill chimneys whose perpetual smoke blackened the stark little gritstone houses for more than a century. The accents you hear are not homespun. They may be of Delhi or of Dallas. For in this unlikely setting, in a four-square parsonage overlooking a graveyard and a bleak, featureless moor, the Brontë sisters lived their brief lives and wrote their eternal books. The lantern in the foreground of the picture hangs on the 'Black Bull' where their brother, Branwell, roystered. The church (rebuilt since the Reverend Brontë's day) and the parsonage are further up the hill, the latter now a well appointed museum. The railway, which was brought up the Worth Valley from Keighley after the Brontës' time, is now preserved as a working museum, with headquarters in Haworth.

CONONLEY

Cononley sits on the River Aire, shortly before it starts its comparatively drab pilgrimage through industrial Yorkshire to join the Ouse. Northwards the prospect is anything but drab a classic example of a glacial valley, fringed by the Drumlins, Skyraikes, Sharphaw and Sugar Loaf, site of wondrous sunsets. The long terrace of stone cottages at the foot of Cononley Brow was known locally as 'Frying Pan Row'. Breakfast used to start early at the bottom house. The communal frying pan was then placed on the flat roof of next-door's privy and so on until all had cooked their eggs and bacon. In Cononley my friend Albert, source of many good tales, was ordered to lop a branch off his ash tree which overhung the traffic, and fulfilled the traditional joke by sitting the wrong side of his saw, with the inevitable result.

THRESHFIELD

'Threshfield for besoms, Thorpe for shoon'. Here, at Ling House, the Ibbotson family for centuries made their celebrated brooms, famed throughout the Riding. The old 'broom age' of Threshfield daily saw two or three horse-drawn wagons, stacked with besoms, ready to leave for the more remote parts of the Dales. We are now in the 'limestone age'; the wagons are more plentiful, not to say insistent. Rose Cottage housed my own family, spanning four generations. The village (the Threshing Field) was founded by the Angles and in the sixteenth century was part of an extensive deer park. The little Elizabethan school, where my father first learnt his tables and beside which my brothers and I used to grub for pig-nuts, is haunted by the ghost and strains of old, crippled Pam the Fiddler, immortalized in Halliwell Sutcliffe's novel.

RYLSTONE

In the bus time-table a lake, in the reality a duckpond, this wayside pool lies serenely in the hollow of Rylstone, the 'Tun by the Rills'. Serenity was shattered in Elizabethan days when the fated Norton family, venerable sire and eight sturdy sons, perished in an attempt to rescue Scottish Mary and restore the Catholic faith. They left their fair sister Emily to mourn with her singular companion – as Wordsworth put it,
 A doe most beautiful, clear white,
 A radiant creature, silver bright.
The ruins of their watchtower stand yet on the moor above. Only one other memorial remains save the legend; a church bell bears the initials J.N. (John Norton) and the family motto, 'God us AYD'. Of their embattled mansion nothing survives but dints and hummocks between the church and the road, covered tenderly every spring by a glorious carpet of snowdrops.

LINTON

Linton-three-bridges, the village by the brook (once the llyn or lake). The road bridge has taken the strain off the ancient pack-horse bridge and beyond these is a primitive span of huge, undressed flagstones. A shallow ford serves the more adventurous. The green is bounded by a 'hospital for indigent women', endowed by one Richard Fountaine, his name perpetuated by the popular little inn. He was a local coffin maker and saw a ready market for his talents in London during the Great Plague. The building expresses his thanks to his god for his preservation from the epidemic and his consequent fortune. Here lived the romantic novelist, Halliwell Sutcliffe, a well of Dales legend and nostalgia. Linton Falls, where the beck reaches the River Wharfe, are an impressive sight and, further downstream, the little, turreted church dates from Saxon times.

GRASSINGTON

Grassington is indisputably the capital of Upper Wharfedale, a compact little maze of cobbled lanes and disparate old stone cottages surrounding the (triangular) Square, once the ancient market place. Bronze and Iron Age villages manifestly thrived here, Druids worshipped in the neighbouring forest and the Roman Eagle surveyed the moorland. Two old cottages mark the bygone barn and theatre where the tragedian, Edmund Kean, once trod the rustic boards. The surrounding hills contain many traces of the flourishing lead mining industry which burrowed beneath them for centuries. The river and Grass Woods overhanging it provide excitement for botanists, naturalists, geologists, artists, anglers and historians alike. Nothing rudely sensational has happened here since the blacksmith, Tom Lee, brutally murdered Richard Petty, the doctor, and was hanged at York in 1766. His body was brought back to hang in chains on Donkey Hill. His smithy and cave can still be seen.

BURNSALL

The comely old church of St Wilfrid's testifies to the antiquity of Burnsall. Anglo-Saxon relics, among them the font, reach back beyond the eighth century. A sturdy, five-arched bridge crosses the River Wharfe to the 'Red Lion', where the recent incumbent of St Wilfrid's could be seen in off-duty moments pulling the pints.
In front is the green with its intermittent maypole – a mystery more pertinent to nearby Thorpe. A little upriver is Loup Scar, riven through massive limestone rock, into which notorious Tom Lee, the Grass Woods murderer, finally hurled his dismembered victim in a sack. St Wilfrid's was, as now, always famous for its bell ringers, and a century ago a string band accompanied the choir. Peter Riley, the Sexton, was adept on the bull fiddle. One evening he shouted excitedly, 'Bill, lad, gie me up some o' that rosin and Ah'll sooin show 'em wheer t'King o'Glory lives!'

HEBDEN

Hebden is the 'Up dene' or high valley; a deep cleavage descending from the high ridge which separates Craven from Nidderdale down to the bed of the Wharfe. Out of the village up Hebden Gill, eventually to Yarnbury and the old lead mines, the lane climbs past Hole Bottom and Jerry and Ben's, where a famed musical family constituted an orchestra in the last century. A gate leads to a picturesque waterfall. The road eastwards to Stump Cross Caverns crosses over the Devil's Bridge. Ralph Calvert was an infamous Thorpe cobbler. Returning from a sales promotion at Fountains Abbey he crossed the flooded ford with difficulty and came upon the Devil. Boldly he shared his eel pie and a bottle of good wine with Old Nick who in appreciation granted him a wish. The bridge was the result and proves the truth of the tale.

THORPE

Hard to find, surrounded by obscuring reef knolls, Thorpe is the hidden village. During the incursions of plundering Scots, Dalesfolk used to flock here for sanctuary. Thorpe once boasted a colony of cobblers who shod the monks of Fountains and the friars of Bolton. They were a lusty crew. One night long ago they stole into Burnsall and made off with the maypole. The Burnsall villagers eventually discovered it, standing tranquilly on the green at Thorpe. To face the shoemakers they enlisted all the neighbouring villages. In a bloody battle the cobblers were decisively thrashed and the maypole was carried back in triumph. Just before the May Day last, the Burnsall maypole once again vanished. As before, a strikingly similar totem appeared on Thorpe green. The drama has not yet been played out. Those anxious for a result must find out for themselves. First find Thorpe.

WATH

In the valley of Upper Nidderdale the road to Wath crosses the Nidd on a narrow, humped packhorse bridge built six centuries ago by the monks of Fountains, marred now for safety by cast-iron railings on the shallowest of parapets. The cottages are, surprisingly, mostly of dressed stone, probably owing to the convenience of a now extinct railway built to serve the construction of Scar House Reservoir, high at the head of the Dale.

Watch Woods, a remaining piece of broad-leaved woodland, Doubergill and Merryfield Glen are rewarding sites for naturalists. The countryside is notable for its great number of fern species, and was especially suited to the growing of flax. Worth a visit is the immense water-wheel on Fosters Beck nearby. Thirty-four feet in diameter and still turning, it drove machinery for the adjacent flax mill as recently as thirty years ago. The mill is now a popular inn.

THORPE

RAMSGILL

The 'Yorke Arms' at Ramsgill with its resident peacock was once a shooting lodge for Gouthwaite Hall, from Elizabethan days the seat of the Yorke family, demolished to make Gouthwaite Reservoir. The family lost favour for harbouring a Gunpowder Plot conspirator, but the events are not connected. Eugene Aram, chronicled scholar and murderer, was born at Ramsgill in 1704. The reservoir, on the River Nidd, is a birdwatcher's Mecca. The last time I passed I was thrilled to see a fishing Osprey from the car. Greenshank, Temminck's Stint, Great Northern Diver, Hobby and Red Kite have all been recorded in recent years, and a Golden Eagle from the Lake District stayed here for three weeks before being found dead on Grassington Moor. Catch the chef of the 'Yorke Arms' in an off-duty moment and he'll tell you the tally in full.

WATH

LOFTHOUSE

Sunset over Stean Moor is seen above rooftops of Lofthouse, high in Nidderdale. Under one, Mrs Thomas, landlady of 'The Crown', was born – she won't say how long ago – and remembers old days and old characters ('There was George Harker; used to get drunk and sleep with the pigs . . .'). She played tenor horn with the band for thirty years. Lofthouse was a grange of Fountains Abbey. Traces remain of bell pits and smelting sites of the monk's lead mines. Now Stean Gorge is a dramatic spot, with accessible caves.
Mrs Thomas was one of three 'postmen' till replaced by a Landrover. As a girl she travelled on the vanished railway. There was no electricity, and water was fetched from the village fountain, which admonishes:
A pint of cold water three times a day
Is the surest way to keep doctor away . . . .

MIDDLESMOOR

Middlesmoor, perched at a dizzy height above the head of the dale, commands spectacular views of the vale of Nidd. The river itself disappears into a cavern two miles above, re-emerging by the old vicarage. The churchyard must boast the most breathtaking vista of any in England. St Chad preached from this eyrie before the Saxon church was built and erected a curious cross which now stands inside by the Norman font. In the old inn, Tom Whitfield, in his nineties doyen of the moorland farmers, claims the vicinity is unparalleled for straight hazel sticks. These modern aluminium crooks turn your hands black and bend when rapped on the ground. As a young'un he played the trumpet with the three Coates brothers in the Midnight Follies Dance Band, travelling to Skipton, Arncliffe and Kettlewell, and always back at dawn for the milking.

KILNSEY

Kilnsey, the 'chilly stream', icy and hard, emerges deep from honeycombed limestone and skirts the village. The Manor House, of ancient frieze and tracery, is crumbling; a Grange built by the monks of Fountains, to which they drove their sheep annually for shearing. Nancy Winter, 'Kilnsey Nan', lived here around 1800, witch and clairvoyant, aided by cards, a divining rod and a guinea pig. Doubtless she starred among the famed wrestlers at Kilnsey Feast which survives as Kilnsey Show in August. So does its daunting Crag Race.

Kilnsey Crag looms massively, its nearness illusory. Amazingly, only prodigious athletes can throw a stone from the road to the crag foot. In childhood I used to wonder where House Martins nested before there were houses. Here's the answer. As Banquo observed, 'No jutty frieze, buttress, nor coign of vantage but this bird hath made his pendent bed and procreant cradle'.

ARNCLIFFE

'Earn Cliff', the eagle rock, once the site of nesting eagles. The pub is, significantly, the 'Falcon', formerly kept by Marmaduke Miller, the noted water-colourist. It's in his family yet, and your ale is still brought up in a jug. The bridge over the River Skirfare and the old tower of the twelfth-century church behind make a charming picture, as does the ancient village, spread around a green, all dominated by unrivalled sweeps of limestone scenery. One of my favourite fishing stories stems from Arncliffe. At a sudden flood, the blacksmith used to desert his anvil, the cobbler toss away his last, the whole village disappear, worm-laden, to the river. Once the Rector, having waited overlong to conduct a funeral, stumped testily to the cottage to find the bereaved housewife greasing the frying pan. 'Nay, Vicar,' she remonstrated, 'Grandad'll wait, but t'fresh wean't!'

FOXUP

Foxup stands at the head of
Littondale. Here Cosh Beck joins
the baby Skirfare to trickle down
the Dale. In parched weather the
water flows underneath the dry
limestone bed. A sudden storm on
Pen-y-Ghent begets a frothing,
peat-stained torrent resembling
cold tea. The motor car can go no
further. Post went daily up to the
now deserted hamlet of Cosh on
horseback. Recently Cosh
provided a refuge for battered
wives. An ideal retreat.
This is a splendid arena for
watching farmer and sheepdog at
work; use of terrain and snap
decisions infinitely more varied
than the formal trials popularized
by television. An old shepherd
once rounded up over a hundred
sheep from a thousand acres of
nearby fell by himself, drove them
up the Dale and safely penned
them at Foxup 'baht dog'!

ARNCLIFFE

GREAT WHERNSIDE

Not a village, but a mountain, rising above Kettlewell to 2,309 feet. This is not the (unqualified) Whernside of the Three Peaks which tops it by more than a hundred feet; the 'Great' distinguishes it from Little Whernside, its partner to the north-east. The name derives from the resemblance in profile to the old 'whern' or 'quern', a stone handmill once used locally for grinding corn into flour. Visible for many miles down Wharfedale and into Airedale, snow on Whernside top is the first indication of the harsh breath of approaching winter. The hill is honeycombed with caves, becks and potholes, and latticed by the ubiquitous dry stone walls, so much part of the landscape one is apt to forget that they were hand-built, every foot of them, by the local shepherds or, in many parts, the old leadminers.

HAWKSWICK

Pretty Hawkswick hides in Littondale, Wordsworth's 'deep fork of Amerdale', sheltered from the rough north winds by a precipitous limestone scar. Below it flows the River Skirfare, soon to mingle with the waters of the Wharfe. Early man lived in nearby Dowkerbottom Cave, up to the fourth century. His lynchets, known locally as 'raines', can be clearly described; terraces cut into the hillside for crop growing. In springtime the surrounding vale is a feast of primroses and wild daffodils, and the woodland full of the scent of lily-of-the-valley.

KETTLEWELL

Where Cam Beck and the Skirfare
join the Wharfe sits 'Ketel's Ville',
mettlesome Kettlewell. Westward
it is shielded by the limestone
ramparts of Knipe Scar,
northward by Tor Mere Top, and
eastward rears the ridge of Great
Whernside. An old coach road
climbs 1,600 feet to Coverdale.
It used to be said that only a
Yorkshireman knows of it, and he
can't find it. Three inns attest to
the ancient standing of Kettlewell,
celebrated for its fairs. St Mary's
Church retains the huge early-
Norman font, decorated with
boars' heads, badges of the Percy
family, and capaciously hewn for
total immersion. Legend holds
that the Clerk and the Sexton used
on Sundays to drive the faithful
with long white sticks from the
pubs to the service, always
refreshing themselves incidentally
with a pot or two of 'yal'. Blessed
are they that thirst before
righteousness!

YOCKENTHWAITE

Little remains of the Forest of
Langstrothdale surrounding
Yockenthwaite. Preserved for the
chase from Norman to Tudor
times, the trees were gradually
felled for agriculture. Further
seedlings are grazed by the sheep
and can establish only in
protecting fissures. Here the
stripling Wharfe has sculpted its
limestone bed into wonderful
shapes and pools. Geese and
ducks need regular access to
water, a ritual known locally as
'sabbling'. Jacky Beresford used to
sabble his geese daily, driving
them here and back in his school
taxi. My grandfather told us many
tales of Yockenthwaite, rarely
visited before cars were plentiful.
To this farmhouse, he alleged,
a couple arrived in some
displeasure. The farmer's wife was
apologetic.
'My man's away up moor wi'sheep.
Can I do owt?'
'I'll come to t'point. Your lad's put
our Mary in t'family way. We've
come about some sort
o'settlement.'
'Nay,' said the woman regretfully,
'I know he charges ten pound for
t'bull and five for t'tup – but what
he'll want for our John, I'd not like
to guess.'

CAM FELL

At the height of Fleet Moss, where
the ancient pack-horse route
between Ribblehead and
Bainbridge crosses the metalled
road between Kettlewell and
Gayle, a forlorn signpost
proclaims 'Cam Houses Only'.
This was once a thriving farming
community. One of the finest
viewpoints in the county, Cam
Fell cradles two infant rivers, the
Wharfe and the Ribble. In
midsummer you will still find
snow in the north-facing gullies;
silhouetted columns of stone are
indeed snow markers, landmarks
for the shepherd when his familiar
world is bland under drifts. On a
good day you can see to witch-
ridden Pendle Hill in distant
Lancashire, the three august
Yorkshire Peaks of Whernside,
Ingleborough and Pen-y-Ghent,
and beyond these the twin pikes
of the Langdales and the Lakeland
mountains. On a poor day, best
stay safe in the valley, for the
weather is treacherous on the
fells, and this is where the weather
is made.

DODD FELL

The Pennine Way marches over Dodd Fell by the West Cam Road, over Rottenstone Hill and down Gaudy Lane to Hawes. The Fell guards the head of Sleddale, the deep valley where Duerley Beck runs into Gayle and Wensleydale. From the car it is best seen from Beggarman's Road, plunging down from the shoulder of Wether Fell. These forgotten ways were busy trade routes centuries ago. Even when I was 'nobbut a lad' there would have been as many haymakers in that field as there are now machine-rolled bales for silage. The dale would have been 'wick wi'folk' at this season, and the farmhouse a bustle of activity.

GAYLE

Make the steep climb up from the head of Wharfedale, over Fleet Moss, crossing the border at the top out of the old West Riding into the North, and you will fall, almost literally, into Wensleydale and the pretty village of Gayle, seen here studying its reflection in Duerley Beck before the waters spill into the River Ure below. This is where the famous Wensleydale cheese (for the Yorkshireman an inspired complement to apple pie) is now mainly made in a small factory founded by the late Kit Calvert (Christopher on Sundays). Kit was Dalesman, raconteur, antiquary, bibliophile and a formidable authority on the Yorkshire dialect. His bookshop in neighbouring Hawes is still a must for booklovers.

A compulsive angling family, we used to take this route regularly when travelling through to fish for trout on the Eden in nearby Westmorland. Traditionally at Gayle we looked out anxiously for geese on the beck and washing on the line. Rarely were we disappointed, and spotting both meant good luck and a full creel. This must have been an unusual day. Perhaps the geese are just upstream and 't'weshin out at back'.

GAYLE

AIRTON

Airton on the River Aire at the approach to Malhamdale is one of the few Dales villages with neither church nor pub. Thirsty travellers up the Pennine Way must trudge on a little further. Handsome seventeenth- and eighteenth-century houses surround the spacious green, which is sliced by a crossroads where the route to Malham is traversed by an attractive cross-country road between Wharfedale and Ribblesdale. The stone posts of the ancient stocks stand on the green and also a seventeenth-century Squatter's Cottage. As it was on common land, a family could settle here temporarily without right or permission. The river below enters a deep pool where there is a mill beside the bridge. Founded by the Canons of Bolton Priory in monastic times, it has now been converted into flats, though its external character is preserved.

HANLITH

Hanlith is a tiny village in a lovely setting, originally founded by the Angles. The Romans seem never to have discovered Malhamdale. Hanlith Hall is late seventeenth century, handsome with stone mullions and imposing clusters of chimneys. Charles Kingsley's little sweep, Tom, lost himself in similar stacks at nearby Malham Tarn before he started anew as a Water Baby in the River Aire. The Pennine Way passes Hanlith on its journey to Malham Cove (Kingsley's 'Harthover Fell'), a phenomenal crescent of limestone cliffs at the base of which the young Aire emerges. Also within easy reach (on foot, for the road peters out at Hanlith) is Gordale Scar, which Turner painted. This is three hundred feet of vertical limestone gorge, once probably a vast cavern which collapsed, where Gordale Beck emerges through a hole near the top, reaching the floor in two awesome cascades.

AIRTON

KIRKBY MALHAM

Malhamdale was, incredibly, isolated until fairly recently and had its distinctive dialect. Prehistoric man found it first. The Anglo-Saxons gave the name Malham. Invading Danes provided Kirkby when the church had stood for a century. The eighth-century St Michael the Archangel is rightly dubbed 'Cathedral of the Dale'. The spaciousness leaves one gasping.. A heavy invasion beam set into the wall could be drawn across the massive door in times of peril. Old box pews bear owners' names or initials, some exquisitely carved. Twice in 1655 a witness to marriages signed himself: 'Oliver Cromwell regd.' Genuine or joke? Thomas Carlyle ridiculed it scathingly, but General Lambert of nearby Calton was the Protector's trusted friend and the church was used as a garrison – witness the empty niches on the ancient pillars where Puritan iconoclasts ran riot. We may never be certain.

GIGGLESWICK

Narrowly separated by the River Ribble from the hectic little town of Settle, Giggleswick is a peaceful contrast of seventeenth-century cottages, a feast of mullions and dripmouldings, stocks and a tithe barn, dominated by the green dome of the chapel of the fifteenth-century Public School. The dome, built to commemorate the Victorian Jubilee, is so familiar a landmark that its incongruity in such a setting goes unheeded in the wealth of sublime mountain scenery.

An ancient market cross stands outside the fifteenth-century church which is dedicated to St Alkelda. She was an Anglo-Saxon princess and martyr, strangled for her faith by the Danes in the twelfth century. The time-worn effigy of Sir Richard Tempest lies in the north aisle. He was buried here in 1488 alongside the head of his favourite horse. The late Russell Harty lived here in Giggleswick.

LAWKLAND

Lawkland is a minute hamlet set in the green farmland just south-west of the Mid-Craven Fault and the busy road to Kendal and the Lake District. The village is dominated by Lawkland Hall, but even this elegant pile is dwarfed by the vista of white limestone scars and the flagships of Ingleborough and Pen-y-Ghent beyond them. The bleached bones of the Pennines are very near the surface. Beside the A65 nearby is the curious Ebbing and Flowing Well at the foot of Buck Haw Brow. It has been integrated with an old stone trough under the trees. The water rises and sinks capriciously; sometimes the well is dry for an hour or more; another time the water might return within a few minutes.

GIGGLESWICK

CLAPHAM

Two great scientists were born at Clapham, both of whom were to influence our heritage. One was Michael Faraday, the physicist, 'father' of electricity; the other Reginald Farrer, the eminent botanist. Farrer's home, Ingleborough Hall, is open to the public, also his famous garden containing many of the hundred new species of plant introduced by him to this country. Fell Beck fills a lake in the grounds and with its picturesque falls, crossed by five bridges, intersects the village. A woodland path leads upstream to Ingleborough Cave, a subterranean fairyland of pillared stalactites and lace-fringed pools. Fell Beck reaches the cave underground. It originates from the distinctive ramparts of Mount Ingleborough, 2,414 feet above sea level, and half-way down plunges into the enormous cavern of Gaping Gill, vast enough to house St Paul's. At certain times of the year the Cave Rescue Association will winch you down in a basket!

AUSTWICK

My grandfather, a keen amateur astronomer, used to tell me of his historic visit to the Game Cock Inn at Austwick on 29 June 1927, from where he climbed Ingleborough with a great company to witness the total eclipse of the sun. The poster advertising the event still hangs in the pub, which on that day was open from 4.00 a.m.

An old Norse settlement and an important market, eventually itself eclipsed by nearby Clapham, the village is a favourite starting-point for climbing the Three Peaks. Austwick Hall is an admirable old house and there is a curious cross on the green. Beside the church stands a grand old sycamore where the one sharp knife in the village used to hang. At a call of 'Whittle to t'tree!', a family could borrow the knife, carve the Sunday roast, and then return it.

HORTON-IN-RIBBLESDALE

Horton-in-Ribblesdale, strung out below the mountainous bulk of Pen-y-Ghent, lowest of the Three Peaks but still attaining 2,273 feet, features in the Domesday survey. The vicarage is the favourite starting-point for climbing Pen-y-Ghent. The most famous of the many potholes burrowing through its limestone, Hull Pot, lies en route. Down in the village the solid little church is Norman. Two lych gates are each roofed with a pair of enormous stone flags. 'Horton Slates', thrown up among the limestone, often on edge, by the upheaval of the Craven Fault, were famous as paving and roofing stone and used locally for building huge rainwater tanks in the farms. Limestone, too, was extensively quarried by the early farmers and burnt with wood (or hereabouts coal, which lay on the surface of the moors) in the circular stone kilns still found dotted about.

STONE HOUSE

The Dales Way passes Stone House at the head of Dentdale, where the River Dee carves a valley between Whernside to the south-west and Great Knoutberry Hill to the north-east. The Dee joins the Rawthey and then the Lune near Sedbergh to reach the sea in Morecambe Bay. Whernside, at 2,419 feet, highest of the Three Peaks, is Yorkshire's second highest mountain. Stone House boasted a renowned marble works, the fossiliferous 'Dent Marble' having once been highly in vogue. Significantly, snow fences edge the fields all the year round in this remote dale. Above, the railway crosses the tall Artengill Viaduct after passing over its longer counterpart at Ribblehead and climbing the mile-and-a-half drag through the Blea Moor Tunnel: astounding feats of engineering skill, built at the cost of so many navigators' lives.

SELSIDE

The Settle-Carlisle Railway skirts the village of Selside a couple of miles before it crosses Batty Moss over the famous Ribblehead Viaduct. Harry Severs was the last signalman. His box has been removed whole and rebuilt in the Carnforth Museum. The sign on the building here looks as though it once graced the box. There is an old range inside and a disintegrating upper floor. This was once styled the Town Hall. From Selside you have a majestic view of Pen-y-Ghent in profile. Diametrically opposite is the path to Alum Pot, a huge gash some three hundred feet deep, approached through a cave called the Long Churn which enters half-way down. Not surprisingly, these potholes housed their ogres. The Boggart of the Pot traditionally lured his victims off the lonely moors to drag them into his lair whence they rarely returned.

APPERSETT

Appersett is astride the Hawes-Sedbergh road where Widdale Beck (happily pronounced 'Widdle') tumbles into the River Ure, draining the ample haunches of Dodd and Widdale Fells. Alternating strata of limestone, shale and sandstone erode and weather at different rates on these hills, the limestone persistent, the sandstone washed and blown away. This is responsible for the stepped silhouettes so characteristic here and for the great number of 'forces' or waterfalls. Hardraw Force, approached through the bar of the 'Green Dragon', is just round the corner from Appersett, where Fossdale Beck leaves Great Shunner Fell to cascade unbroken for over one hundred feet. A slippery path climbs up between the scar and the waterfall and you can stand behind and see the sunshine through this incredible curtain. Turner painted it. Wordsworth and Ruskin praised it. I saw it in the 1947 winter – a single, titanic icicle.

HAWES

A meshwork of narrow streets and
the little 'capital' of Upper
Wensleydale, Hawes is Yorkshire's
highest market town by a charter
granted by William III in 1699. It
is both tourist centre (the Pennine
Way passes through) and farming
centre. The broad valley of the
Dale is ideal for dairy-farming.
Sadly the once common
Wensleydale sheep, large, pale
and hornless, their high-ridged
foreheads lending them a haughty
look of disdain, are now so thin on
the ground as almost to have
reached rare-breed status. Hawes
has a rewarding craft centre in
'The Neukin', once the site of the
'Padding Can', a fourpenny doss-
house. Hawes Junction (now
renamed Garsdale) on the Settle-
Carlisle Railway is one of the
loneliest stations in an area famed
for them. An engine on a turntable
was once blown completely
tender-about-face by the force of
the wind.

BURTERSETT

The road out of Burtersett on the flanks of Wether Fell commands one of the best panoramic views of Wensleydale spread out below. Though the name 'Yoredale' will be met sparsely, this is the one major dale not named after its river, the Ure.

The eponymous little village of Wensley houses a candle factory, its wares exquisitely decorative, but the best practical candles were made at Burtersett by Candle Willie in the old silk mill. Billy Tommy Willie Metcalfe made candles and tallow dips, straight and of even thickness, for the farmers' wives and for the quarrymen working underground in the drifts.

The fields between village and quarry are crossed by stone-flagged paths, relics of the days when angry farmers complained that the constant tramping was ruining good grazing land and hay meadows. Wild meadow flowers still grow here in profusion.

MARSETT

I last visited Marsett, in Raydale, remote at the head of Semerwater, on the summer solstice, which for reasons I can never remember is not midsummer's day. Blue Meadow Cranesbill and white Queen Anne's Lace were rampant, and the air was fragrant with the Pernod flavour of Sweet Cicely. The lake lay still and serene, though I have known it suddenly steel-grey and cruel, lashed into waves by an angry gale. Only a small batch of sheep farms and the mandatory holiday cottages, Marsett yet has its chapel with a fine holly tree. Improbably on this day it was full and heavy with glorious scarlet berries, exactly six months out of season.

COUNTERSETT

The numerous '-setts' in Wensleydale derive from the Scandinavian *seters*, farms used for hill grazing during the summer. The Norse settlers must have been thankful to find terrain like their own native land where there was also sheltered low country to house their stock in winter. Countersett Hall dates from 1650, a charming old stone house with a handsome tripartite window, the top sheltered by a hoodmould. The picture looks over the village, nestling in the hollow where the River Bain leaves Semerwater, towards the heights of Wether Fell.

STALLING BUSK

This is a sheep farm, one of the small cluster of buildings at Stalling Busk above the wide bowl of Semerwater, the only natural lake in Yorkshire. Beyond is the ridge of Bardale. A curious old ruined chapel has a bell turret projecting beyond the gable. Semerwater is a classic example of a glacial lake, but according to legend a town stood here. A weary traveller begged shelter from a raging storm but none would succour him save one poor farmstead. On his departure he cursed the town, decreeing that it should be drowned under rushing waters. Except for the hospitable farmhouse, the lake covered every dwelling. There is evidence of a Bronze Age settlement having occupied the lake, so the story could have its roots in folk-memory. Until recently a haven for wildlife and waterfowl, Semerwater has been discovered as a playground.

BAINBRIDGE

At the end of the first century AD the Romans built a road from Ilkley to Bainbridge, and a wooden fort on Brough Hill. Here the Bain, the shortest (named) river in England, brings the waters of Lake Semerwater down some lovely falls to the River Ure. Addleborough provides the backcloth. Set round a broad green complete with old stocks and millstones, the village has no church, but George Fox, the great Quaker, used to preach at the Meeting House. Many of the old houses retain outside stone steps to the upper storeys. The fifteenth-century 'Rose and Crown' is keeper of the Forest Horn. Although the forest has disappeared, the mighty horn is still blown by the Metcalfe family of a winter's evening from Hawes Back-end Fair at Holyrood until Pancake Tuesday at Shrovetide, to spur 'the lated traveller apace to gain the timely inn'.

ASKRIGG

The most northerly clearing up the Dales made by the Angles became enchanting Askrigg, inspiration for *A Yorkshire Village* by Marie Hartley and Joan Ingleby. More recent fame came with television's *All Creatures Great and Small*, for 'Skeldale House' is opposite the thirteenth-century church. Less passively, Askrigg was noted for hand knitting and clock making. In 1688 Kit Atherstone was fined by the Archdeacon's Court for hanging out his stockings on the Sabbath. An ancient bull-baiting ring is still set in the square next to the stepped market cross and a cylindrical stone pump. On my last visit I chatted with Roy Kneeshaw on the steps of his eighteenth-century Elm House while he clacked industriously away on his spinning-wheel. North from Askrigg the mountain pass climbs into Swaledale; nothing for miles but wild moorland. Mill Gill is close by, falling some seventy feet, and the Lady's Slipper Orchid hides here. Sea pinks cover Askrigg Common. What more can one ask?

SEDBUSK

The southern flank of Great Shunner Fell, Yorkshire's fourth highest mountain, sweeps down to Stag's Fell, sheltering the high pasture and the village of Sedbusk, a huddle of pretty stone cottages around a green with a magnificent copper beech. Building stone was always in plentiful supply, for the village is surrounded by old, disused quarries; healed scars where nature has largely reclaimed its own. Sandstone was hewn out of the rock and brought down by ponies, while powerful shire horses hauled huge slabs which used often to slide down with a perilous momentum of their own, to the now dismantled railway which ran the length of Wensleydale from Hawes Junction. It is appropriate that present-day holidaymakers can avail themselves of the nearby pony-trekking centre.

THWAITE

A barn at Thwaite, as yet unconverted. There aren't many left. Over the road is the Kearton Guest House where you can get a good old-fashioned Yorkshire 'high tea'. Cherry Kearton and his brother, Richard, were born at Thwaite, sons of a shepherd and gamekeeper, and became internationally famous as the first pioneers of wildlife photography. The village was nearly totally washed away in a great flood down the fell side at the end of the nineteenth century.

The road from Hawes crosses high over Abbotside Common into Swaledale, arriving at Thwaite, via the famous Buttertubs Pass. These are deep, fern-lined, columnar holes in the limestone. Remote and isolated before the advent of the motor car, the Buttertubs' reputation rather outsoared the reality. As one shepherd described them, 'Some on 'em's bottomless – and some's deeper'n that!'

MUKER

On the green foot of Kisdon the
little village of Muker, its grey
houses seated one on top of
another and crowned by the
sixteenth-century church, has
depended on sheep for its
prosperity since the era of the big
monasteries and probably well
before that. 'A terrible sheep man'
is the highest commendation for a
Swaledale farmer. Traditional
hand-knitting is still maintained
at Muker, a flourishing cottage
industry.

The remoter dales have never
neglected music or the arts.
Witness the charming little mid-
Victorian Literary Institute with
its tubby gable. Notable Muker
folk, the Guy family and their
relatives still constitute a highly
successful silver band which,
among more august venues,
compete *al fresco* at the natural
rocky amphitheatre at Hardraw in
Wensleydale. The 'Farmers Arms'
remains an unassuming village
pub despite the enormous influx
of visitors in recent years. Out of
season it is still a farmers' pub,
given to good ale, a warm hearth,
gossip, darts and dominoes.

ANGRAM

Angram, at 1,185 feet above sea level, is the highest village in Yorkshire, on the route to the Tan Hill Inn, the highest pub in Britain, where the famous annual Tup Show is held. A good tup (ram) will fetch four figures. 'Swardle Yows' (Swaledale ewes) are the tough, horned, black-faced, grey-nosed breed seen grazing all over the Yorkshire Moors.

Here you look over the gate at curious Kisdon Hill, almost an island between the encircling Swale and Muker Beck. Behind you is the cottage of the late Bill Alderson, 'Bill Up t'Steps', farmer, councillor and wit. His robust steps are now out of true and his cottage sadly derelict. A travelling rep once complained,
'It's a long road to your house!'
'Aye,' was the terse reply. 'It is that! If it were ony shorter, it'ud not reach!'

LANGTHWAITE

Langthwaite is the principal village in Arkengarthdale, a dale which clanks with Viking shields and battleaxes in village names such as Whaw, Wham, Windegg, Eskeleth and Booze. Since the Romans the dale was a thriving lead mining centre. Windsor Castle and the Bloody Tower were roofed with local lead. A little six-sided powder house still stands at Langthwaite. The water splash, the little bridge and the hospitable 'Red Lion' will be recognized straightaway from the regular opening sequence of *All Creatures Great and Small*. Before television? The landlord is understandably nostalgic. 'The youngsters don't stay. We used to have a cricket team; football; concerts; plays – the Village Hall had a grand stage.' The Village Hall is now up for sale as a holiday cottage.

CASTLE BOLTON

The village is a single street of stone cottages under Bolton Castle, open to the public, magnificently four-square, true to every schoolboy's image of a medieval fortress. Built by Richard Scrope, Richard II's Chancellor, and licensed in 1379, it surveys and guards the length of Wensleydale. In 1568 Mary Queen of Scots spent an unhappy time here in 'honourable custody', knitting and hunting. She was assisted to escape, but lost her shawl in her flight over the moor to Leyburn, which led to her recapture. The hilly ridge is still known as 'The Shawl'. The castle was besieged by Cromwell during the Civil War. In the gruesome dungeon the bones of an arm were discovered, still fettered to the wall by an iron ring.

GRINTON

The Corpse Way finishes its melancholy trail at St Andrew's, Grinton, early Norman 'Cathedral of the Dale', the roomy church of one of the widest parishes in England. The dead were carried here on men's shoulders in relays from villages far up Swaledale, in rough wicker baskets, a perilous journey in times of flood. In the seventeenth century, to stimulate the woollen trade, the law decreed that the dead should be buried in wool. Anne Barker was buried here in 1692 in a linen shroud, and her father was consequently fined five pounds. In every shepherd's coffin a fleece was laid. This badge is to authenticate his profession on Judgement Day and thus obtain him pardon for his sporadic attendances at church.

GAMMERSGILL

'Where my caravan has rested,
Flowers I leave you on the grass.'
This one has rested here as long as
I can remember. Whispers of our
book have got round and it has
been given a coat of paint. Too
late! You might not find
Gammersgill on the road map.
The tiny hamlet sits between
Carlton and Horsehouse in lonely
Coverdale. Though niggardly as a
caravan site, the scenery is
breathtaking whichever way you
look. Beyond the River Cover are
the remains of Coverham Abbey
and a fascinating nursery which
specializes in rare alpines. This
pastoral setting bore Miles
Coverdale, whose English
translation first made the Bible
available to the common people
four-and-a-half centuries ago.

HORSEHOUSE

Horsehouse is in Coverdale, up-dale of the racing stables of Middleham. The true Dalesman knows his horseflesh. A Dales proverb advises, 'Shake a bridle o'er a Yorkshireman's grave and he'll rise up and steal your horse.' George Borrow was hardly more polite: 'Trust a cat among cream, but never trust a Yorkshireman in the saddle of a good horse.' At Horsehouse the London-Richmond mail coach used to rest the horses overnight after climbing the tortuous one-in-four gradient of Park Rash out of Kettlewell, a stern test even for cars today. The horses were stabled in what is now the tap-room of the 'Thwaite Arms'. Seen here in St Botolph's churchyard, overloomed by Penhill (a beacon hill during the Napoleonic wars), towers a rare and impressive Weeping Beech, a mighty veteran of at least two centuries, a cathedral of a tree.

BRADLEY

On the maps, Bradley; to the residents of Coverdale, 'Braidley', which has a broad, warm Yorkshire resonance. Like 'graidely!' This is 'Back o' Bill Lambert's at Braidley'. That should be set to music. Below it the River Cover threads a course through gouged ravines north-east into Wensleydale. Little Whernside rises steeply on the other side. It is a wild country, bleak, spacious and empty, the grass and bracken furrowed by narrow ghylls and waterfalls and populated by few save the tough moorland sheep. No wonder that travellers on the London-Richmond mail were advised to settle their affairs before they undertook the journey!

WEST SCRAFTON

Steep lanes climb to West Scrafton from the River Cover. Beyond rise Carlton Moor and Pen Hill, stronghold it is said of a giant that ravaged the countryside long ago. The village is a close gathering of old houses round a minuscule green, jealously guarded by small stone posts and chains. Behind, Roova Crag beetles over the village above West Scrafton Moor, where there is an outworked coal-mine. Local coal was once fairly plentiful and was used to fuel the lime kilns once the ancient woodland had been burnt. Quicklime was spread on the 'intake' land and slaked by the rain, changing the nature of the soil and allowing pasturage to grow where bracken and heather had flourished. It is no accident that on the lower side of an enclosing wall you stand on green grass but look over it on to coarse moorland.

BELLERBY

Bellerby Beck runs through this pretty village below the garden gates, filled with wild yellow monkey-musk, crossed by stone flag bridges to gain access to the cottages. It skirts the village green and a sturdy sycamore growing from a pair of steps, and flows in front of the fine Old Hall with its gabled porch and mullioned windows. At one end of the village the sixteenth-century Manor House is now a farm. Above Bellerby you have a splendid view to the east of the gentler Vale of York and the distant Hambleton Hills.

LOW BURTON

In the church behind the broad market square at Masham stands a monument to Sir Marmaduke Wyvill, 1613, sleeping near his wife, their children kneeling below. The brevity of their fragile span is emphasized in the spandrels by Father Time and a cherub, eloquently blowing soap bubbles. The Wyvills lived here at Low Burton Hall. An earlier Sir Marmaduke left his initials in 1548. The historic hall has stood in part since the thirteenth century, no doubt then among farm buildings as it does today. Low Burton marks the sudden, dramatic change in scenery from the harsh fells of Wensleydale to the fertile arable plain of York.

WELL

Well is a tranquil village, just off the road between Masham and Thirsk. The original well was known to travellers before the Romans arrived. The Romans built a villa here and bits of tesselated pavement have been found. Red 'Roman' pantiled roofs replace the prevalent sandstone flags, the 'grey slate' of the Dales. It is said that stones from the villa were originally used to build the mainly medieval church, resting-place of the influential Neville family, the Lords Latimer. Certainly the warm, mellow stone is very old, the same material used in a beautiful row of almshouses which lead from the old lych gate. These were founded by Lord Ralph Neville, six hundred years ago. Sir John Neville accompanied Henry VIII on his last visit to France. The Bluff King Hal eventually married one of Sir John's stepmothers, the widowed Catherine Parr, who was lucky enough to outlive her sovereign lord. Today the old cottages and their gardens are a delight.

LAVERTON

Snug at the very eastern foot of the Pennines among small villages with sonorous names, Galphay and Grewelthorpe and Kirkby Malzeard, the hamlet of Laverton is reached by tree-screened lanes over a little hump-backed bridge spanning the River Laver as it runs off Dallowgill Moor. Near the Methodist chapel there is an airy barn and shop given over to the drying of ferns, flowers and grasses. It is almost possible to rule a line here where the dry stone walls abruptly finish and fence and thorn hedge enclose the fields instead; fields sown with oats, barley and wheat as the moorland grazing gives way to the fecund plain surrounding Fountains Abbey, tilled centuries ago by monks and still productive today.

CARLTON HUSTHWAITE

A quiet village, its old houses are predominantly of weathered red brick, set alongside a green shaded by two aristocratic trees, a beech and a horse chestnut. The church is older, seventeenth century, of an ochreous brown stone with a stumpy tower capped by a flat pyramid. Nearby is Carlton Hall behind its own green. Opposite the hall, and in striking contrast, stands a grand old black-and-white house, thatched and half-timbered. Further from the church an old manor house, its crumbled brick covered in creepers, completes the restful scene. From the village the White Horse of Kilburn, high on the Hambletons just south of Sutton Bank, is eyecatching. Of no great antiquity, the horse, which illustrates local legends, was carved in the turf in the middle of the nineteenth century by a team under the direction of the village schoolmaster. Twenty people, it is said, can sit on its eye.

COXWOLD

Laurence Sterne, eccentric author of *Tristram Shandy*, was vicar of Coxwold in the 1760s, and Shandy Hall where he wrote and the church where he preached are packed with history and interest. The latter contains much treasure and decoration, including original fifteenth-century glass and a 'Breeches' Bible of 1601, framed in a case by Thompson, the mouse-man. From here the neat, broad village street slopes downhill between greens and cobbles and houses of pale buff-grey stone below red 'Roman' pantiles, characteristic features of villages from here to the east coast. The old grammar school dates from James I's accession and quaint almshouses, the Fauconberg Hospital, from the reign of his grandson, Charles II, as does the fine old inn, the Fauconberg Arms. Thomas, Earl Fauconberg, married Mary Cromwell, the Lord Protector's daughter. Early in the Restoration, Cromwell's cadaver was torn from Westminster Abbey, hanged at Tyburn and beheaded. Mary is believed to have retrieved her father's body, sans head, and secretly walled it up here in an attic at Newburgh Priory.

CARLTON HUSTHWAITE

NUNNINGTON

Nunnington hides above a loop of the River Rye. The greens fronting the houses undulate in close-mown emerald humps; a ghost is said to haunt an avenue of imposing sycamores which climbs the hill. The National Trust administers Nunnington Hall and its riverside gardens, built on the site of an old nunnery, since Stuart times the home of Viscount Preston and the Grahams. Here is displayed the intricately furnished Carlisle Collection of Miniature Rooms. In the hilltop church a carved dragon decorates one fragment of a tenth-century stone cross. The effigy of Sir Walter Teye (1325) lies in a recess, armour-clad, his legs crossed (sign of a crusader), and a lion crouches at his feet. That's the official line, anyway. The village knows he is really Sir Peter Loschi, one of King Arthur's knights, and his fearless mastiff. They both perished ridding Nunnington of a Loathly Worm which had long ravaged the countryside and carried off the prettiest virgins to its dragon's lair on Loschy Hill.

RIEVAULX

Higher up towards the head of Ryedale stands Rievaulx (Rye Vale) Abbey. 'Bolton for the artist, Fountains for the historian, Rievaulx for the poet.' It inspired both Cowper and Wordsworth, though Cotman, Girtin and Turner all painted this Cistercian foundation, which rivals Tintern for beauty. Colonized in 1131 and completed in the mid-thirteenth century, it is marvellously preserved, second only to Fountains. The surroundings are breathtaking, a deep, narrow cleft in wooded crags. The Cistercians habitually built their abbeys near plentiful water; the more savage the site, the better favoured. The associated little church had to be built, because of the terrain, north to south instead of the conventional east to west, a source of superstition and alarm. A contemporary chronicler described this grandiose setting as 'a place of horror and waste solitude'.

HAWNBY

Hawnby's red-roofed cottages are gathered on the side of distinctive Hawnby Hill far up Ryedale above its abbey, reached by a route scarcely rivalled for its scenic beauty. The River Seph joins the Rye below. The village street squeezes narrowly between farmhouses, and the little church is surrounded by woodland sloping down to the river. A charming feature to the left of the simple altar is a painted memorial tablet to Anne Tankard, who died in 1608 in her second year. She is depicted asleep in her cradle by a lily and a rosebush, with a clock, tellingly stopped between one and two. Her grandfather, Raife, who survived her nearly twenty years, dying at 73, is on a similar tablet on the right. An hour-glass has run through; he completed his allotted span of three-score years and ten.

RIEVAULX

HAWNBY

FADMOOR

Fadmoor is just north of Kirkbymoorside and the busy Thirsk-Scarborough road, at the approach to Farndale, valley of the River Dove. A reposeful village of well-loved cottage gardens and small orchards, it is fetchingly representative of lowland villages under the North Yorkshire Moors. The 'Plough Inn', which pulls a grand pint of ale, overlooks the wide green, shaded by sycamore and horse chestnut, the whole surrounded by farms and long, low barns and meadows given to hay. In summertime the fields are liberally scattered with scarlet poppies.

LOWNA

Lowna Bridge crosses the River Dove among the alder trees and farms of this tiny hamlet. The white track is Lund Road, climbing northwards out of Farndale past Hangman Stone to the height of Blakey Rigg. Lowna is associated with a well-known witch, Nan Hardwicke. Folk were amazed by the speed she travelled until it was discovered that she crossed the moors as a hare. Cruck-framed, thatched houses are scattered among the cottages in Farndale. Two curved timbers were arched and fastened at the top to make a cruck. A cross bracing timber formed the letter 'A'. Such frames were linked, ten to twelve feet apart, by a horizontal roof tree and joined at the base by low stone side walls with spars from their tops to the ridge, the 'riggin'. The bays so formed were of the breadth required to stall a pair of oxen.

LOW MILL

Low Mill is even further up, nestling in the hillside on the western edge of Farndale. The pantiled roofs make an intricate pattern of varying heights and angles, and where can you find a more delectable post office? The chapel (1901) bears in its wall memorial stones to Featherstones, Wasses, Tinsleys and Breckons, old Sunday School scholars. Old mounting blocks enhance old barns and a thatched, cruck-framed cottage still stands. The chimney would originally have been a headless barrel in the thatch, lined with clay, over an open fire on the floor beneath. Bishop Hall described such a farmer's house as

Of one bay's breadth, God, what a silly cote!
Whose thatchèd spars are furred with sluttish soote
A whole inch thick, shining like blackmoor's brows.
At his bed's feet feeden his stallèd teame,
His swine beneath, his pullets o'er the beame.

FARNDALE

There is no village of Farndale. The name is given to the whole lovely valley of the River Dove. Farndale is famous for its indigenous wild daffodils in springtime, golden masses of Lenten Lilies, to give them their old Yorkshire name. They are now protected by the National Park. Once a car, laden to the gunwales with daffodils, stopped a local farmer.

'Can I take this road to Pickering?' He was told, 'Aye, tha might as weel. Tha's tekken nigh on everything else!'

A sprite associated especially with Farndale is the Hob. Hairy elves, hobs worked on farms, requiring no reward but a nightly jug of cream. Jonathan Gray of Farndale inherited a highly industrious hob and he became most prosperous. Sadly, after his wife's untimely death, Gray remarried. His new spouse was so mean that she begrudged even the nightly cream. Resenting a diet of skimmed milk, the hob turned his energies to mischief and malevolence and soon, near to ruin, the farmer secretively packed all up to move away from the dale and the hob. A neighbour stopped him on the way.

'Nay! Tha's not flittin?' On the cart a wizened brown face peered from under a milk churn lid. 'Aye, we're flittin!' said the hob.

HUTTON-LE-HOLE

'By Hammer and Hand, All Arts do stand'. So states the legend on the lintel of the former inn at Hutton-le-Hole, an allusion to the iron mining which once overspread the moors around. Hutton-le-Hole is in Ryedale, astride a cleft carved by Hutton Beck, crossed and recrossed by little white-railed bridges from a wide village green, closely trimmed by black-faced sheep.

The village was once a refuge for persecuted Quakers. John Richard was a friend of William Penn, toured North America on a white horse, preached to the Red Indians and helped to found Pennsylvania. He returned to this haven to end his days in his seventeenth-century Quaker cottage.

A supremely helpful information centre forms the threshold of the Ryedale Folk Museum, almost a village of its own, its houses graphically reliving the customs, trades and crafts of the past four hundred years.

ROSEDALE

The road nor-nor-east from
Hutton-le-Hole climbs the length
of the high ridge separating
Farndale from its eastward
companion, Rosedale, valley of
the River Seven. At the head of
Rosedale it loops in a great arc to
travel down the other side
through vast sweeps of
grousemoor and heather,
a shimmering, purple sea in late
summer. Half-way down is
Rosedale Abbey, a village built on
the site, and probably with the
stones, of a twelfth-century
nunnery. Little of it remains. The
old lintel above the church door
proclaims, 'All is Vanity'. Also
vanished, more recently, is the
chimney of the old ironstone
mine, once a landmark from afar.
The Dale has its share of pagan
denizens. Hobb Crag and Hobb
Farm speak for themselves. Aud
Esther Mudd o'Rosedale had the
evil eye. In a round barrow on
Loose How, a coffin was found
containing a clothed body with an
early Bronze Age dagger, and a
stone battleaxe.

BECK HOLE

Beck Hole is just that. Approached
down a one-in-four knife edge
from Goathland, the village nests
in a deep tree-filled hollow where
Wheeldale Beck and the curiously
named Murk Esk join to run
northwards into Eskdale. One
runs through green pasture, the
other off the moorland peat, and
in times of flood two distinct
streams, one green, the other dark
brown, run side by side in the
river. Once a boom village, with
ironstone mines and two blast
furnaces, Beck Hole lies on the
original route of the Whitby-
Pickering Railway. At first, horses
pulled the coaches up the steep
incline. The homely little Birch
Hall Inn (an alehouse of some
centuries' standing, it once
advertised its wares with a
traditional birch bush) now has
for its sign a large, dramatic,
Turneresque oil-painting of the
beck and ravine from the bridge
by Algernon Newton, RA.

RUNSWICK BAY

Climb out of Beck Hole up on to
Fylingdales Moor, turning your
back on the surrealistic giant golf
balls, and the route becomes a
coastal road to Whitby and
beyond. The fishing village of
Runswick clings (not always
securely in its past) to the high
cliffs sheltering the west of
Runswick Bay, looking eastwards
to Kettleness. The lifeboat has a
brave history; on one occasion it
was manned entirely by the
women-folk when their men had
been caught by a freak squall.
The shifting cliffs constantly
reveal new fossils. A century ago
the remains of plesiosaurus and
ichthyosaurus were discovered
here and ammonites abound,
locked in small ironstone pebbles
scattered on the beach. At night
you might hear the faëry Bogles of
Claymore Well, washing and
bleaching their clothes and
welting them rhythmically with
battledores, long wooden paddles
eventually superseded by the
mangle.

STAITHES

On the road, near the highest point on the English coast, the village seems disappointing, but leave the car, as you must, and walk down the steep hill to the old village. 'Steears' to the locals, it hides between two bulky headlands, home to generations of fisherfolk whose dwindling cobles still bob below the harbour. The older women, unselfconsciously, wear their traditional white bonnets, black on Sundays. They are friendly folk – ever since their ancient forebears ill-treated a pair of stranded mermaids, who rewarded them with a disastrous flood. Precipitous cobbled lanes tumble between the houses, names such as Gunn Gutter, Slip Top and Dog Loup – the last, at eighteen inches wide, the narrowest street in the North of England. Captain Cook was apprenticed here to Mr Sanderson, Grocer and Draper, before he ran away to sea at Whitby. The old shop was washed clean away along with a dozen other cottages by the savage North Sea in 1745. The 'Cod and Lobster Inn' has been rebuilt several times, victim of the storms. John Paul Jones landed on a foraging raid in 1779, and many press-ganged 'Steearsmen' were killed at Trafalgar.

ROBIN HOOD'S BAY

The bay is guarded by high headlands; North Cheek, or Ness Point and South Cheek, Old Peak. At the summit of the village the red-roofed houses appear to overhang the cliff. At the bottom they encroach on the sea wall itself, so near that at times the tide thunders up the street and the bowsprit of a ship is reputed to have crashed through the windows of a pub. A flavour of sea-wrack, tarred rope and kippers, a pastiche of figureheads, drying nets, crab-pots and lines and an intimation of salty yarns and smugglers' holes combine to make this the most picturesque fishing village of this picturesque coast. The sea is both lifeline and enemy. In 1881, the storm raging too fiercely at Whitby to put out, the lifeboat was dragged agonizingly over the moors and let down these cliffs to rescue six fishermen.

NEWTON-UPON-RAWCLIFFE

Back inland towards Pickering, Newton-upon-Rawcliffe is approached through tree-bordered lanes, past a field covered by a large flock of barnyard geese, honking defiantly as though Christmas will never come. The hedge bottoms are allowed to run riot with grasses and wild flowers. A wide dewpond on the village green is home to a score of farmyard ducks, and opposite is the Mel House Bird and Animal Garden, where the children can feed the lambs or romp exotically with rheas and wallabies, terrapins and Sebastopol geese, and charming Vietnamese Pot-Bellied Pigs.

ROBIN HOOD'S BAY

APPLETON-LE-MOORS

Climbing north from the main road between Kirbymoorside and Wrelton over Spaunton Moor brings you to Appleton-le-Moors, its long, broad High Street bordered by the customary lawns in front of the houses, several of them handsome, three-bayed Georgian buildings. The rather ornate church was designed in thirteenth-century style by the architect of Truro Cathedral. Its tower and spire are visible for long distances when the trees are bare. The late Victorian village hall has a charming conical bell turret reminiscent of Snow White's castle. Sheep roam freely all over the High Street. They keep the greens beautifully short, but watch out for the divots!

LOCKTON

Lockton is set high on the moors above a wooded, deeply channelled glen, with a distant view of the spherical, puffball growths of the Fylingdales early warning establishment. Its green is transected by a crossroads and populated by guineafowl and muscovy duck. Although today it boasts a Youth Hostel, the village has an old-time logic, mainly disparate old stone cottages with varying levels of roofs, with the Rectory at one end, the Church at the other end and the Squire in the middle. The grey church is medieval with a squat fifteenth-century tower out of which for a hundred years an ash tree used to grow – now gone, but long the 'cynosure of neighbouring eyes'.

THORNTON DALE

Thornton-*le*-Dale when I was a lad, and styled the 'Prettiest-Village-in-Yorkshire', though who flings down these gauntlet pronouncements I can't surmise. I shall take no sides, but it certainly ranks high among the most bonny. At one end are an ancient market cross and old stocks on the village green. Thornton Beck curves through the village and little humped bridges cross it from the Malton road, allowing one to reach Rose Cottage, Ivy Cottage, Brooklet Cottage and their companions dryshod. The Tudor hall is set among copper beech and chestnut, and a humbler, earlier, cruck-framed thatched cottage still stands. The single-storey almshouses, culminating in the taller Grammar School, are mid seventeenth century. In the churchyard sleeps Matthew Grimes, who died in 1875 at ninety-six, a veteran of the Peninsular War. As a guard on St Helena, he helped to carry Napoleon to his grave.

LOCKTON

OLD MALTON

To the south of Pickering the road leads down to the flat plain where the many dales rivers are gathered by the Derwent to skirt the Howardian Hills. Here is lovely Old Malton, village of old stone. The imposing church originated in a Gilbertine Priory, built in the mid twelfth century and flourishing until the Dissolution. Some of its furniture is by Robert Thompson of Kilburn, whose first commission was in Hubberholme Church in Wharfedale. As he was then 'as poor as a church mouse', his little carved mouse adorns all his work. In the churchyard lies Charles Smithson, lawyer and close friend of Dickens. Together they invented a schoolboy destined for a Yorkshire boarding school. Posing as a prospective parent, the novelist did his research for *Nicholas Nickleby*. The timbered, pewter-hung, sixteenth-century 'Royal Oak' was a permitted haunt, in the 1940s, of German and Italian POWs. Some still return to visit Mine Host, the genial Tony Upsall, plumber, artist, trombonist and Victorian Weight Lifter.

LANGTON

A few miles further south into the fertile Yorkshire Wolds, country lanes wind to Langton, a little village of considerable charm. Although the original 'Lanton' features in the Domesday Book, the present village was built almost entirely over two decades early in the nineteenth century, a regular but informal arrangement of pale stone cottages all with pointed windows and arched doorways. The church is older, with a thirteenth-century font and some Jacobean panelling. Near the altar is a monument to Mrs Ingram, who died in 1656 giving birth to twins who didn't survive. Their painted figures lie beneath a long, eulogistic poem, the babes tightly swathed, their heads pillowed disturbingly on little skulls. An eminent authority describes her as a 'recumbent effigy, a little stiff'. I'm certain the pun was unintentional.

WHARRAM-LE-STREET

Passing from Langton through the village of Birdsall you reach Wharram-le-Street on the way to Wetwang. You are now in racehorse country, in lanes where the hedge verges in high summer are aglow with cornflower and scabious, meadow brown butterflies flap lazily among the tall grasses, and little flocks of goldfinches flash as they rise from the seed heads.

One of the largest round barrows in Britain is near here on Duggleby Howe. Fifty late Stone Age cremation burials, with bone and flint tools, all occurred at the same time – perhaps the result of a battle? Next door Wharram Percy is a deserted medieval village.

LANGTON

SLEDMERE

Sledmere, an orderly conglomerate of neat red brick and bright red paint, is almost a memorial to the Sykes family, originally sixteenth-century Leeds merchants. Sledmere House was started by Sir Richard Sykes in 1751. Sir Christopher completed it in the 1780s. His memorial, a Tuscan rotunda, incorporates the village well and commemorates his phenomenal agricultural achievements. A pseudo Gothic tower on the hill honours the first Sir Tatton, renowned bare-knuckle fighter, who founded the famed Sledmere Stud. This enterprise was developed by Sir Tatton, his son, who also built his own and many neighbouring village churches. He instigated a copy of an Eleanor Cross, now a war memorial. A special memorial was designed by Sir Mark Sykes, to his own company of Wagoners, a corps of some thousand farm workers who provided horse-drawn supply transport to the First World War trenches for one pound a year. The eighteenth-century coaching inn, the 'Triton', is still licensed to let post horses.

TIBTHORPE

From Sledmere, Tibthorpe lies
beyond the deliciously named
Wetwang, among fields of wheat
and barley, a peaceful tribute to
the foresight of Sir Christopher
Sykes, who 'set such an example
to other owners of land as had
caused what was once a blank and
barren tract of country to become
now one of the most productive
and best cultivated districts in the
county of York'. The village is a
row of farms and small Georgian
houses, mellow red brick and
pantiles. There is no village pub,
but the village shop, 'which sells
owt', provides a lively centre for
grapevine and gossip.

WARTER

Just short of Pocklington is
Warter, a trim little village with a
triangular village green, a
duckpond with an island and a
church with a spire. Apart from
the supremely pretty row of
thatched cottages, most of the
houses, though diverse, are staid
and Victorian with lovingly
clipped hedges. Even the iron
street lamps are wistfully
Victorian.
Londesborough Park adjoins the
village, once the home of George
Hudson, the Railway King, in his
heyday. Long before on this site,
Henry Lord Clifford spent his
boyhood incognito, hidden from
his enemies of the House of York,
in the guise of a simple farmer's
son. He eventually returned to
Skipton Castle as the Shepherd
Laird.

KIRBY UNDERDALE

In a leafy setting, the school
bounds one end of the broad
village street, the other leading to
the hills. The interesting little
church below might have heard
the din of two great battles. At first
sight it appears curiously to have
dormer windows in the roof.
Within, one finds that these serve
to let light into the nave. When
first built at the time of the
Conquest it was a smaller edifice,
less high and with no aisle, joining
the west tower seen in the picture.
From the hill above Kirby
Underdale you have a view of six
dales. The two battlefields lie
westward on the plain, with York
between: Stamford Bridge to the
fore and Marston Moor more
distant, where Englishmen shed
the blood of Englishmen on the
English earth and each, though six
centuries separated them, changed
history and led shortly to the
death of an English King.